THE INTERNET SAFETY HANDBOOK

INVESTIGATE!

KEEP YOUR SOCIAL NETWORK SAFE

BY CHARLEY LIGHT

Enslow PUBLISHING

Please visit our website, www.enslow.com. For a free color catalog of all our high-quality books, call toll free 1-800-398-2504 or fax 1-877-980-4454.

Library of Congress Cataloging-in-Publication Data

Names: Light, Charley, author.
Title: Keep your social network safe / Charley Light.
Description: Buffalo, New York : Enslow Publishing, [2024] | Series: The Internet safety handbook | Includes index. | Audience: Grades 2-3
Identifiers: LCCN 2023008325 (print) | LCCN 2023008326 (ebook) | ISBN 9781978535138 (library binding) | ISBN 9781978535121 (paperback) | ISBN 9781978535145 (ebook)
Subjects: LCSH: Internet and children–Juvenile literature. | Social media–Juvenile literature. | Internet–Safety measures–Juvenile literature.
Classification: LCC HQ784.I58 L54 2024 (print) | LCC HQ784.I58 (ebook) | DDC 004.67/8083–dc23/eng/20230410
LC record available at https://lccn.loc.gov/2023008325
LC ebook record available at https://lccn.loc.gov/2023008326

Published in 2024 by
Enslow Publishing
2544 Clinton Street
Buffalo, NY 14224

Portions of this work were originally authored by Barbara M. Linde and published as *Safe Social Networking*. All new material in this edition authored by Charley Light.

Designer: Jen Schoembs
Editor: Charley Light

Photo credits: Cover (girl), p. 1 (girl) Rawpixel.com/Shutterstock.com; cover (background), p. 1, series art (background) kerly chonglor/Shutterstock.com; p. 5 Gladskikh Tatiana/Shutterstock.com; pp. 7, 11 Prostock-studio/Shutterstock.com;p p. 15, 25 Monkey Business Images/Shutterstock.com; p. 17 GOLFX/Shutterstock.com; p. 19 Africa Studio/Shutterstock.com; p. 21 wavebreakmedia/Shutterstock.com; p. 23 Ground Picture/Shutterstock.com; p. 27 RUCHUDA BOONPLIEN/Shutterstock.com; p. 29 New Africa/Shutterstock.com.

Printed in the United States of America

CPSIA compliance information: Batch #CSENS24: For further information contact Enslow Publishing at 1-800-398-2504.

CONTENTS

Words in the glossary appear in **bold** type the first time they are used in the text.

SOCIAL SPIDERS

You've heard of social butterflies, but social networking is more like being a spider at the center of your own web. But what is a social network?

A social network is a group of people who have their own relationships with each other. Your family is one social network! Everyone at your school makes up another social network. When you put all your social networks together, you can see the big web of people you are connected to! With a guardian's permission, you can spin a social network on the World Wide Web too.

Social networking can help kids stay in touch with family members who live far away.

EXPLORE MORE

Ever wonder what the "www" at the beginning of a website's name stands for? It means "World Wide Web"! This is a big web of information that people can access on the internet. You can search for info on a **web browser.**

SOCIAL NETWORKING SITES

Social networking sites are places online where people can communicate with each other. YouTube, TikTok, Snapchat, Facebook, and Twitter are all social networking sites. People can also **socialize** through online games such as *Minecraft* and *Fortnite*.

To use a social networking site (with the help of a trusted adult), you make a profile. This usually includes a username (your name on the site), a profile picture, and information about yourself. You can become friends with other users. It's easy to send messages, share photos and videos, and sometimes chat over a video or a voice call.

EXPLORE MORE

Age requirements for social networking are different around the world. In the United States, you should be at least 13 to use most social media and online games. In some European countries, you should be at least 16.

You should be at least 13 and have a guardian's permission to post your videos on YouTube.

OUTSIDE YOUR WEB

All your connections on the internet make up your online social network. This can include people you know in person and new friends you meet online.

When you share information about yourself online, anyone can find it—even people outside your social web. Once something is posted—a photo, a full name, a home address, a message—it can never be fully deleted. People in your social web can share your information too. Something you text to a friend could end up being posted on **social media**.

MAKE YOUR OWN SOCIAL SPIDER WEB

This exercise can help you understand how information moves through social networks.

What You'll Need:

- Paper
- Pen or pencil

Instructions:

- Draw a circle in the middle of a piece of paper and put your name in it.
- Now write the names of each of your friends in surrounding circles.
- Draw a line from your name to each friend's name.
- If your friends also know each other, draw lines to connect their names.

Think About It:

Imagine you send a picture to a group chat with all your friends in this web. Each of your friends has their own social web they could share your picture with too. Before you share anything, be sure it is something that would be safe for all these people—and even strangers—to see.

EXPLORE MORE

The first social network was SixDegrees.com. It launched, or went online, in 1997. Users could make their own profiles, make friends on the site, and send messages to each other. It was mostly used by high school students and young adults.

TERMS OF SERVICE

Each social networking site has a set of rules that tell what behaviors aren't allowed. This is usually called the terms of service. Most terms of service usually don't allow posting harmful photos, language, or content.

Before joining a site, you usually have to read the terms of service and click in a box to show that you agree to the terms. If you don't accept them, you can't fully use the website. If you do accept the terms and then disobey them, you might have your account removed.

EXPLORE MORE

Terms of service can also include who owns the content (photos, videos, text posts, and so on). Sometimes the terms say that the website owns anything you post there. That means they can use your content how they want without paying you.

Always have a guardian help you make social media accounts. Read the terms of service together.

UNIQUE USERNAMES

Your username is the name everyone on a social networking site will see. Make sure you don't put any private information in your username, like your full name, age, home address, or even your email address. Don't use special numbers such as your birthday or your jersey number.

It can be hard to think of a username that isn't already taken. Try combining different things you like, such as favorite colors, foods, sports, or movies. You can also change the spelling to make your username unique. Sometimes you can use special characters like an underscore (_).

MAKING A SAFE USERNAME

	dangerous	risky	SAFE!
username	Zoe42James	ZooPlaysHockey	HockeyWolf
safety score	This one has your full name and your hockey jersey number (42). This is *way too much* private info!	This one uses your real life nickname (Zoo). Still a bit too risky.	You decide to pair your favorite sport with your favorite animal. No private info, and still very *you!*

Let's pretend your name is Zoe James and you are trying to make a safe username. See which possible username is the safest!

EXPLORE MORE

If you make more than one social media account, make different usernames for each site. That way, people cannot recognize you from one site on another site. You should have a different password for each site too.

PASSWORD DON'TS

Your password is like a key that unlocks the door to your social media account. It should be a combination of letters, numbers, and characters (like !@#%?). It usually needs at least one capital letter too.

The trick is making a password you can remember, but others can't guess. Just like your username, you shouldn't use any private information. Also, don't put anything from your username in your password. If Zoe's username is HockeyWolf, their password shouldn't have "Hockey" or "Wolf" in it. It's best not to use full words you can find in a dictionary.

EXPLORE MORE

Use different passwords for each place you need one. Change your passwords often. Never share your password with friends or other people. They could use your account without your permission. You could get in trouble for their actions on your account.

It's okay to share your passwords with your guardian.

PASSWORD DOS

There are so many things *not* to put in a password! So, how do you actually make one? Do use a mix of lower- and uppercase letters. Use random numbers. Make up words or phrases. Get creative!

Try writing a phrase you like on paper, such as "You scream, I scream, we all scream for ice cream!" Now take some random letters from that phrase. Add some random numbers and special characters. You could make something like: "Ys2mI*re7iC!" (But don't use that, or anyone who reads this book will know it too!)

EXPLORE MORE

Some web browsers will make a password for you. This will usually look like a random string of characters. Browsers can also remember passwords for you too. This is less secure, or safe, than typing in your password yourself.

You can write down your usernames and passwords in a safe notebook to remember them.

PRIVACY SETTINGS

Protecting your privacy helps keep your social web safe. Each social networking site has privacy settings. Kids and teens should always keep theirs at the highest level of privacy. That means your information cannot be viewed by just anyone. You decide who your friends are on each social network. You decide which of those friends can see some or all of your information.

Remember, online posts are never completely private. Always ask permission from other people before posting photos or messages about them. Ask your friends to do the same for you.

Once a photo is posted online, people can always find it again, even if it is taken down.

EXPLORE MORE

Most social media sites allow tagging, or labeling, people in posted photos. Your privacy settings should let you know when someone tags you. You can say no to being tagged. You can also ask the person to take the photo down or ask the site for help.

PROFILES

Your profile is your place to share who you are. It usually includes a space called "About Me" where—you guessed it—you write about yourself!

You can be yourself and keep important information private at the same time. Don't share where you go to school or your home address. Don't share specific places you go, like the name of a park you go to every weekend. Don't include contact information such as a phone number or email address. If you aren't sure if something is safe to share, talk to your guardian first.

EXPLORE MORE

Sometimes people pretend to be someone they are not online. Adults can even pretend to be kids. They may even try to get kids to meet them in person. If someone online asks you for private information, tell a guardian or adult you trust.

Some apps can share your current location with friends. Turn off location sharing in privacy settings.

UNKIND ONLINE

It's always important to be kind. Online, your words and actions can last forever. It's extra important to think twice before you say or do something that could hurt other people online.

Cyberbullying is when people use digital **technology** to bully, or purposefully hurt, other people. The most effective way to protect yourself from cyberbullying is to **block** people who are being hurtful. You can also **report** people cyberbullying to the website. Never cyberbully back—that just hurts more people and can get you in trouble too. Talk to an adult you trust if you feel unsafe.

EXPLORE MORE

When you are in an email with multiple people, there is an option to click on "Reply" or "Reply All." Clicking "Reply" will send your message to one person. "Reply All" sends your email to the whole group.

Cyberbullying hurts everyone that's part of it—those being bullied, the people who see it, and the person cyberbullying.

There are other kinds of bullying behaviors, or actions, to watch out for in your online social network. Trolling is posting hurtful attacks on **message boards** or other group sites. It can include changing the subject being talked about to something unhelpful or hurtful on purpose.

Griefing is purposefully bothering other players in online multiplayer games. These are games with multiple players. The biggest are massive multiplayer online (MMO) games and can have millions of users. Griefing may include placing obstacles in other people's paths, sending nasty messages, or killing other characters in an unfair way.

Minecraft lets players talk to each other through text online.

EXPLORE MORE

When you're ready to get rid of technology such as phones, computers, laptops, or even gaming devices, make sure you delete all of your private information first. You can usually click "Restore to Factory Settings" to delete everything from the device.

SOCIAL NETWORKING FOR SCHOOL

Some schools use social networking to help students learn. During the **COVID-19 pandemic**, many schools around the world had to teach their students online. In the United States, 93 percent of homes with kids in school had to participate in online learning in 2020 (the first year of the pandemic).

Brainly, Edublogs, and Minecraft Education are some of the social networking sites made for students. They help students learn and work together. These sites have rules to keep students safe. You should still ask a guardian for permission to use them.

EXPLORE MORE

In the United States, up to 16 million students didn't have the tools they needed to learn online in 2020. Up to 400,000 teachers didn't have the tools to teach online from their homes, either.

Relationships—offline and online—are an important part of learning.

SAFE SPIDERS

Talk to an adult you trust about a safety plan for your online social web, if you have one. Social networking sites can change often, so decide together how to keep track of changes happening online.

Check your privacy settings often. Look at the permissions social networking apps ask to use. Make sure no apps are using your camera, microphone, or location unless there's a good reason. You should be able to control when apps can use these things. With help from a trusted adult, your web can stay safe online and off.

There are lots of ways to stay connected to your social web offline.

EXPLORE MORE

Lots of families connect on social networks. Your guardians might use social media and maybe even post about you too. You can talk to your family and friends about **boundaries** with social media. This keeps everyone comfortable and safe.

GLOSSARY

block: To turn on a setting that stops another user from being able to see your profile or talk to you.

boundaries: The ways a person wants to be treated, their limits, and treatment they will not accept from others.

COVID-19 pandemic: A global spreading of the COVID-19 virus that forced most people to stay inside their own homes for a time.

message boards: A place online where people can make posts on topics and reply to each other.

report: Telling a website that another user is behaving harmfully.

socialize: To interact with other people.

social media: Websites and applications, also known as apps, used to create online communities.

technology: Using science, engineering, and other industries to invent useful tools or to solve problems. Also a machine, piece of equipment, or method created by technology.

web browser: A program for finding and reading websites on the internet.

FOR MORE INFORMATION

BOOKS

Beam, Bjorn. *Security Squad: Your Kid's Playbook to Cybersecurity, Cyberbullying, and Coding!* Chicago, IL: Beam Reach Ventures, 2019.

Grant, Joyce. *Can You Believe It?: How to Spot Fake News and Find the Facts.* Toronto, ON: Kids Can Press, 2022.

Newman, Catherine. *What Can I Say?: A Kid's Guide to Super-Useful Social Skills to Help You Get Along and Express Yourself.* North Adams, MA: Storey Publishing, LLC, 2022.

WEBSITES

Brainly
brainly.com
Get help with schoolwork from fellow students around the world!

Dinopass
www.dinopass.com
This cool site for kids will make simple and strong passwords for you!

Edublogs
edublogs.org
With a guardian's permission and help, you can create a free blog here.

Publisher's note to educators and parents: Our editors have carefully reviewed these websites to ensure that they are suitable for students. Many websites change frequently, however, and we cannot guarantee that a site's future contents will continue to meet our high standards of quality and educational value. Be advised that students should be closely supervised whenever they access the internet.

INDEX